CW00346744

You are
MAGICAL

summersdale

YOU ARE MAGICAL

Compiled by Holly Brook-Piper and Jess Zahra

An Hachette UK Company
www.hachette.co.uk

Summersdale Publishers Ltd
Part of Octopus Publishing Group Limited
Carmelite House
50 Victoria Embankment
LONDON
EC4Y 0DZ
UK

www.summersdale.com

Printed and bound in Poland

ISBN: 978-1-83799-451-9

Substantial discounts on bulk quantities of Summersdale books are available to corporations, professional associations and other organizations. For details contact general enquiries: telephone: +44 (0) 1243 771107 or email: enquiries@summersdale.com.

TO..

FROM..

INTRODUCTION

Congratulations, you are now
the proud owner of this groovy
collection of positive messages!

These inspiring quotes and pearls of
wisdom from famous thinkers and modern
superstars alike have been carefully
curated to lift your vibe, while the selection
of empowering affirmations will help you
embrace your own unique brilliance.

Whether you need to cast off your
self-doubt, stand firm in times of challenge
and change, or simply give yourself
the recognition you deserve, open this
book on any page to spark your joy.

**Stay fearless and believe in yourself
– because you are magical!**

HAVE FAITH IN THE MAGIC AND MIRACLES OF LIFE, FOR ONLY THOSE THAT DO GET TO EXPERIENCE THEM.

HAL ELROD

if you
really want
something,
you can
figure out
how to make
it happen.

CHER

THE WORLD IS
BETTER
WITH ME IN IT

WHO WANTS TO BE NORMAL WHEN YOU CAN BE UNIQUE?

HELENA BONHAM CARTER

I HAVE COMPASSION FOR MYSELF AND OTHERS

ONCE YOU MAKE A DECISION, THE UNIVERSE CONSPIRES TO MAKE IT HAPPEN.

RALPH WALDO EMERSON

When I'm not feeling my best I ask myself, "What are you gonna do about it?" I use the negativity to fuel the transformation into a better me.

BEYONCÉ

I AM
WORTHY
OF
LOVE

You have to
be unique, and
different, and shine
in your own way.

LADY GAGA

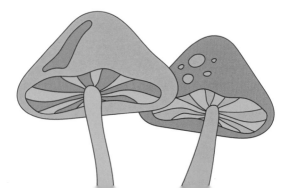

I
BELIEVE
IN
MYSELF

Nothing really matters except what you do

NOW

in this instant of time.

EILEEN CADDY

I RADIATE POSITIVE ENERGY

KEEPING BUSY AND MAKING OPTIMISM A WAY OF LIFE CAN RESTORE YOUR FAITH IN YOURSELF.

LUCILLE BALL

I AM IN TUNE WITH MYSELF AND ALL OTHER LIVING BEINGS AROUND ME

**IT'S NEVER
TOO LATE TO BE
WHAT YOU MIGHT
HAVE BEEN.**

GEORGE ELIOT

SOMETIMES YOU'VE GOT TO LET GO OF THE GOOD TO MAKE WAY FOR THE GREAT!

LIVE ALL
YOU CAN;
IT'S A MISTAKE
NOT TO.

HENRY JAMES

I LET MY
IMAGINATION
SOAR

BE PATIENT AND TRUST THE UNIVERSE. EVERYTHING HAPPENS FOR A REASON AND YOU WILL BE OKAY.

ARIANA GRANDE

I DEFINE WHAT SUCCESS MEANS TO ME

OUR life is shaped by OUR mind; we become what we think.

BUDDHA

I WILL SEIZE JOY EVERYWHERE I CAN

THINK OF ALL THE BEAUTY STILL LEFT AROUND YOU AND BE HAPPY.

ANNE FRANK

If we treated
ourselves the way
we treated our
best friend, can
you imagine how
much better off
we would be?

MEGHAN, DUCHESS OF SUSSEX

I AM CONFIDENT THAT I HAVE THE POWER TO CHANGE MY LIFE

The universe buries strange jewels deep within us all, and then stands back to see if we can find them.

ELIZABETH GILBERT

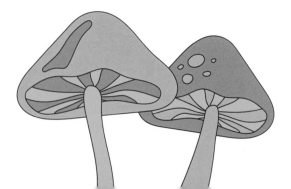

I WELCOME REJUVENATION OF MY MIND, BODY AND SOUL

There are **TALKERS** enough among us; I'll be one of the **DOERS.**

CHARLES DICKENS

FOLLOW YOUR BLISS, AND THE UNIVERSE WILL OPEN DOORS WHERE THERE WERE ONLY WALLS.

JOSEPH CAMPBELL

THERE IS POWER AND POSSIBILITY WITHIN ME

**YOUR PRESENT
CIRCUMSTANCES DON'T
DETERMINE WHERE
YOU CAN GO; THEY
MERELY DETERMINE
WHERE YOU START.**

NIDO QUBEIN

KEEP YOUR HEAD UP

LEARN MORE ABOUT YOURSELF AND FALL MORE IN LOVE WITH YOURSELF EVERY DAY.

ZENDAYA

i am deliberate and afraid of nothing.

AUDRE LORDE

I BELONG HERE

Believe you can and you're halfway there.

THEODORE ROOSEVELT

I AM
OPEN TO
HEALING

EVERYTHING YOU CAN IMAGINE IS REAL.

PABLO PICASSO

To the mind
that is still, the
whole universe
surrenders.

LAO TZU

I WELCOME MENTAL CLARITY

Once you replace
negative thoughts
with positive ones,
you'll start having
positive results.

WILLIE NELSON

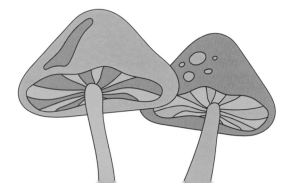

I DESERVE
TO TAKE
UP SPACE

SELF-CARE
means giving yourself
PERMISSION
to
PAUSE.

CECILIA TRAN

I EMBRACE
CHANGE

LIFE ISN'T ABOUT FINDING YOURSELF. LIFE IS ABOUT CREATING YOURSELF.

GEORGE BERNARD SHAW

I VOW TO BE KIND TO MYSELF EACH AND EVERY DAY

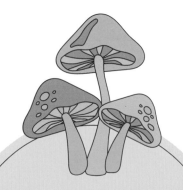

GET TO THE DEEPER BUSINESS OF BEING BEAUTIFUL INSIDE.

LUPITA NYONG'O

MY PERSPECTIVE IS UNIQUE AND IMPORTANT

TO LOVE ONESELF IS THE BEGINNING OF A LIFELONG ROMANCE.

OSCAR WILDE

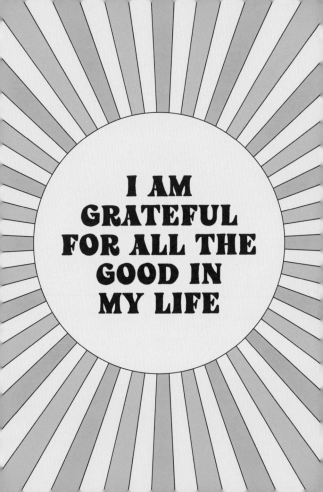

EVERYTHING
YOU WANT ALSO
WANTS YOU.
BUT YOU HAVE
TO TAKE ACTION
TO GET IT.

JACK CANFIELD

I AM A
STRONG,
CAPABLE
PERSON

SELF-LOVE HAS VERY LITTLE TO DO WITH HOW YOU FEEL ABOUT YOUR OUTER SELF. IT'S ABOUT ACCEPTING ALL OF YOURSELF.

TYRA BANKS

I FORGIVE MYSELF, AND I FREE MYSELF

ONLY THOSE WHO WILL RISK GOING TOO FAR CAN POSSIBLY FIND OUT HOW FAR ONE CAN GO.

T. S. ELIOT

MY PAST
DOESN'T
DICTATE MY
FUTURE

Nothing can
dim the light
which shines
from within.

MAYA ANGELOU

NEGATIVITY HAS NO HOLD OVER ME

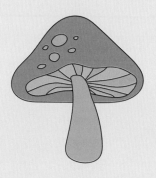

Self-compassion is simply giving the same kindness to ourselves that we would give to others.

CHRISTOPHER GERMER

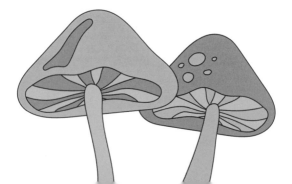

TODAY I WILL DO MY BEST

I believe that
if you'll just
STAND UP
and go,
life will
OPEN UP
for you.

TINA TURNER

WHEN YOU VISUALIZE, THEN YOU MATERIALIZE. IF YOU'VE BEEN THERE IN YOUR MIND, YOU'LL GO THERE IN YOUR BODY.

DENIS WAITLEY

I TRUST MY
INTUITION

FIND YOUR OWN STYLE AND HAVE THE COURAGE TO STICK TO IT.

JOAN CRAWFORD

I AM AT PEACE WITH MYSELF

TALK TO YOURSELF LIKE YOU WOULD TO SOMEONE YOU LOVE.

BRENÉ BROWN

TO ACCOMPLISH GREAT THINGS WE MUST NOT ONLY ACT, BUT ALSO DREAM; NOT ONLY PLAN, BUT ALSO BELIEVE.

ANATOLE FRANCE

I CAN DO
ANYTHING
I PUT MY
MIND TO

THE ONE THING THAT YOU HAVE THAT NOBODY ELSE HAS IS YOU.

NEIL GAIMAN

I ATTRACT ABUNDANCE INTO MY LIFE

I HAVE INSECURITIES, OF COURSE, BUT I DON'T HANG OUT WITH ANYONE WHO POINTS THEM OUT TO ME.

ADELE

I WELCOME
NEW
ADVENTURES

The main
requirement for
spiritual growth:
a yearning to know
who you really are.

ADYASHANTI

NO AMOUNT
OF WORRYING CAN
CHANGE
THE FUTURE

Go boldly and honestly through the world. Learn to love the fact that there is nobody else quite like you.

DANIEL RADCLIFFE

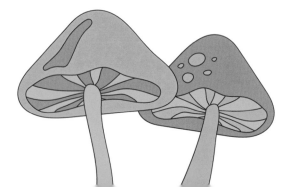

MY
MISTAKES
DO NOT
DEFINE ME

There is
nothing
either good
or bad, but
THINKING
makes it so.

WILLIAM SHAKESPEARE

I GIVE
MYSELF
PERMISSION
TO REST

I TRY
TO AVOID
LOOKING
FORWARD OR
BACKWARD,
AND TRY TO
KEEP LOOKING
UPWARD.

CHARLOTTE BRONTË

I TAKE CARE OF MY BODY AND IT TAKES CARE OF ME

HOPE IS
A WAKING
DREAM.

ARISTOTLE

I PRIORITIZE MY WELL-BEING

IT'S ALL ABOUT WHAT MAKES YOU FEEL GOOD.

BILLIE EILISH

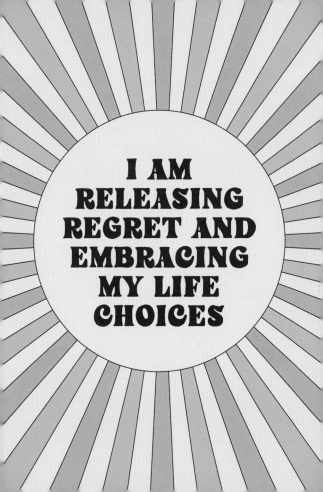

TO FREE US
FROM THE
EXPECTATIONS
OF OTHERS, TO
GIVE US BACK
TO OURSELVES –
THERE LIES THE
GREAT, SINGULAR
POWER OF
SELF-RESPECT.

JOAN DIDION

I CHOOSE
HAPPINESS

YOU GET IN LIFE
WHAT YOU HAVE
THE COURAGE
TO ASK FOR.

OPRAH WINFREY

I OPEN MY HEART TO NEW OPPORTUNITIES

THE CHALLENGE IS NOT TO BE PERFECT, IT'S TO BE WHOLE.

JANE FONDA

It's important not
to limit yourself.
You can do whatever
you really love to do,
no matter what it is.

RYAN GOSLING

I AM IN CONTROL OF MY DESTINY

May you live every day of your life.

JONATHAN SWIFT

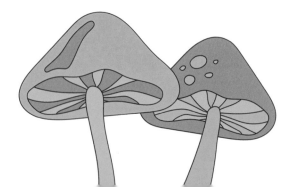

I HAVE THE COURAGE TO ACHIEVE MY GOALS

Keep your
MIND FIXED
on what you
WANT IN LIFE:
not on what
you don't want.

NAPOLEON HILL

WHETHER YOU COME FROM A COUNCIL ESTATE OR A COUNTRY ESTATE, YOUR SUCCESS WILL BE DETERMINED BY YOUR OWN CONFIDENCE AND FORTITUDE.

MICHELLE OBAMA

I AM
SAFE
AND
SECURE

EVERY SINGLE SECOND IS AN OPPORTUNITY TO CHANGE YOUR LIFE.

RHONDA BYRNE

I AM
A GOOD
PERSON

I AM ALWAYS IN QUEST OF BEING OPEN TO WHAT THE UNIVERSE WILL BRING ME.

JILL BOLTE TAYLOR

THROW YOUR DREAM INTO SPACE LIKE A KITE, AND YOU DO NOT KNOW WHAT IT WILL BRING BACK, A NEW LIFE, A NEW FRIEND, A NEW LOVE.

ANAÏS NIN

I BELIEVE IN A
BRIGHTER
FUTURE

THERE ARE BETTER THINGS AHEAD THAN ANY WE LEAVE BEHIND.

C. S. LEWIS

GOOD
THINGS
ARE
HAPPENING

I KNOW MY STRONG POINTS: I WORK HARD, I HAVE TALENT, I'M FUNNY AND I'M A GOOD PERSON.

PINK

I AM THE CREATOR OF MY BEST REALITY

There is no way
to be perfect
and no fun in
being perfect.

ALICIA KEYS

I AM
HONEST
WITH MYSELF
AND OTHERS

You already have within you everything you need to turn your dreams into reality.

WALLACE D. WATTLES

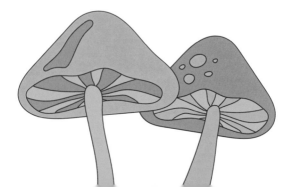

I AM OPEN TO PERSONAL GROWTH

The secret
to doing
anything is
BELIEVING
that you
can do it.

BOB ROSS

ALWAYS GO WITH YOUR PASSIONS. NEVER ASK YOURSELF IF IT'S REALISTIC OR NOT.

DEEPAK CHOPRA

I WILL
MANIFEST
THE LIFE OF
MY
DREAMS

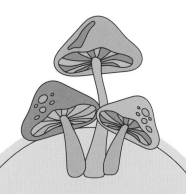

IF YOU'RE PRESENTING YOURSELF WITH CONFIDENCE, YOU CAN PULL OFF PRETTY MUCH ANYTHING.

KATY PERRY

I TRUST THAT I AM ON THE RIGHT PATH

THERE IS ONLY
ONE CORNER OF
THE UNIVERSE YOU
CAN BE CERTAIN
OF IMPROVING,
AND THAT'S YOUR
OWN SELF.

ALDOUS HUXLEY

ONE DAY
AT A TIME,
ONE STEP
AT A TIME

FEAR KILLS YOUR ABILITY TO SEE BEAUTY. YOU HAVE TO GET BEYOND FEAR.

WILL SMITH

I AM
NOT
AFRAID
TO
SHINE

DON'T SIT
DOWN AND
WAIT FOR THE
OPPORTUNITIES
TO COME.
GET UP AND
MAKE THEM.

MADAM C. J. WALKER

I
CHOOSE
HOPE

GO CONFIDENTLY IN THE DIRECTION OF YOUR DREAMS. LIVE THE LIFE YOU'VE IMAGINED.

HENRY DAVID THOREAU

Thoughts become things. If you see it in your mind, you will hold it in your hand.

BOB PROCTOR

I PUT MY
ENERGY
INTO
THINGS THAT
MATTER
TO ME

Sometimes the smallest step in the right direction ends up being the biggest step of your life.

EMMA STONE

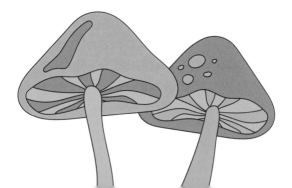

I AM
EXCELLENT
AT WHAT
I DO

You've got to **VALUE YOURSELF** and know that you're worth **EVERYTHING.**

JENNIFER LOPEZ

I CAN
TAKE DEEP
BREATHS

IF YOU HAVE A POSITIVE FRAME OF MIND, YOU CAN MANIFEST POSITIVE THINGS IN YOUR LIFE.

ALESHA DIXON

I AM
POWERFUL

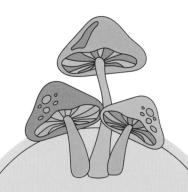

THE MAIN PERSON YOU HAVE TO TRICK INTO CONFIDENCE IS YOURSELF.

ZADIE SMITH

I CAN
DO
THIS!

DON'T FEEL
STUPID IF YOU
DON'T LIKE
WHAT EVERYONE
ELSE PRETENDS
TO LOVE.

EMMA WATSON

HOWEVER difficult life may seem, there's always something you can do and succeed at.

STEPHEN HAWKING

MY MIND IS FULL OF BRILLIANT IDEAS

SET YOUR GOALS HIGH, AND DON'T STOP TILL YOU GET THERE.

BO JACKSON

I AM
MAGICAL

PUT YOUR SHOULDERS BACK AND CHIN UP, AND FACE THE WORLD WITH PRIDE.

HELEN MIRREN

FINAL WORD

Now you have experienced the power of these pick-me-ups and feel-good vibes, you have opened a portal to a deep, enriching and loving relationship with yourself.

Celebrate your unique power, because when you do, you are sure to feel nothing less than magical!

Manifest Your Way to Happiness

All the Tips, Tricks and Techniques You Need to Manifest Your Dream Life

Hardback

ISBN: 978-1-80007-917-5

Trust in the universe and it will deliver

Manifestation is one of the most powerful tools we have at our disposal, and the good news is that anyone can try it – the universe is ready and waiting to help you achieve your goals, realize your dreams and live your best life. By harnessing your positive energy through techniques such as visualization and scripting, you can communicate your desires to the universe and start working towards attaining them.

It's time to start changing your life through the power of your mind!

Positive Mental Gratitude

Quotes and Affirmations to Help You Appreciate the Good Things in Life

Hardback

ISBN: 978-1-80007-836-9

Positive Mental Gratitude is your go-to guide to harnessing the power of positive thought, and will help you to relish the small pleasures, be kind to your mind and brighten your world. Spilling over with beautiful quotes on the practice of gratitude, it will empower you to celebrate the present, even in times of challenge and change.

Have you enjoyed this book?
If so, find us on Facebook at
Summersdale Publishers, on Twitter
at **@Summersdale** and on Instagram
and TikTok at **@summersdalebooks** and
get in touch. We'd love to hear from you!

www.summersdale.com

Image credits

Cover and throughout © EnkaArt/Shutterstock.com;
pp.4-5 and throughout © Pensiri/Shutterstock.com;
p.7 and throughout © Chief Design/Shutterstock.com

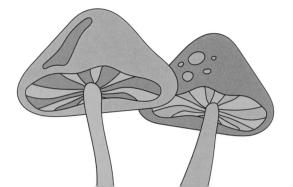